Fatma Karmostaji was born and raised in Dubai, UAE. She began writing at the age of 13, using her middle school projects and her love for literature as a way to express her creativity in writing. Although she grew up to major in Accounting and Finance, she continued feeding her creativity through reading and analyzing various books in both Arabic and English, which ignited her love for poetry. *She Found Blue* is her first book.

To my parents and sister
who were always my biggest supporters

And to the young girl
who allowed me to share her story
in the way I sought fit...

Thank you.

Fatma Karmostaji

SHE FOUND BLUE

AUSTIN MACAULEY PUBLISHERS®

LONDON • CAMBRIDGE • NEW YORK • SHARJAH

ISBN – 9789948732686 – (Paperback)
ISBN – 9789948732679– (E-Book)

Application Number: MC-10-01-6723176
Age Classification: 17+

The age group that matches the content of the books has been classified according to the age classification system issued by the UAE Media Council.

Printer Name: iPrint Global Ltd
Printer Address: Witchford, England

First Published 2024
AUSTIN MACAULEY PUBLISHERS FZE
Sharjah Publishing City
P.O. Box [519201]
Sharjah, UAE
www.austinmacauley.ae
+971 655 95 202

Firstly, I want to thank my mom and dad, for always pushing me to go after what I want in life. Although I did not pursue writing and literature in university, my parents always reminded me to never let go of my love for reading and writing. They reminded me that your hobbies can put your skills to tremendous use, and that skills are meant to be developed and not abandoned.

I want to thank my sister, Manal, for always supporting me and keeping me in her prayers. She was my diamond throughout my process of writing this book, and I will forever be grateful for all the encouragement she offered me. She was a person I constantly looked up to for strength, and it is her courage and strength that pushed me to share my writing with the world.

I also want to thank my close circle of friends who showed interest in my writing and lent a listening ear to the same. I could not have done it without their support and kind words.

I want to thank the wonderful team at Austin Macauley Publishers for giving me the opportunity to share my writing with the rest of the world. They assigned a wonderful team to help me achieve my dream and make my vision a reality. Finally, I want to thank all of you, my wonderful readers, who purchased this book and are about to embark on this journey of emotions with the protagonist. To be able to share this with all of you fills me with great joy.

Table of Contents

Chapter 1: The Beginning   **13**

Swing   *15*

Diamond   *18*

Yellow   *20*

Moon   *21*

Butterfly   *23*

Cloud   *25*

Sunstone   *27*

Chapter 2: The First   **29**

Love   *31*

Souls   *34*

Hers   *37*

Hurt   *41*

Rain   *44*

Why?   *47*

Chapter 3: The Inevitable   **51**

Bubble   *53*

Flames   *55*

Dust   *58*

Pain   *60*

Maybe   *63*

Red   *65*

Sealed   *67*

Heart   *69*

Fear   *72*

Hail   *75*

Lost   *78*

Attached   *80*

Snow   *83*

Numb   *86*

Stars   *89*

Destroy   *91*

Used   *94*

Time   *97*

Third   *99*

Limit   *102*

Chapter 4: The Rebirth   **105**

    Grey   *107*

    Ocean   *109*

    Snake   *111*

    Bird   *114*

    Blue   *117*

Chapter 1
The Beginning

Swing

At the mere age of six,
She ran barefoot on the sandy beaches of the country,
By the crystal blue water as the wind blew her two braids.

An innocent smile decorated her blushed face
As her father carried her and took her to where the swing swayed.

She screamed in glee as her mother pushed her back and forth,
In awe of how the cold kissed her skin, but a sense of warmth settled within.
She was living every child's innocent dream,
Hoping it would never end but rather repeat all over again.

That was the earliest memory that settled itself within her brain,
That was the last time she recalled being utterly carefree,
Hoping she could relive it all over again.

She grew up to see her father's smile still mark his once
wrinkle free face.
She grew up to hear her mother's concerned tone, still
hugging her like a warm embrace.

Time was their worst enemy, she realized,
As anxiety crawled its way into her head.
Time was her worst enemy, she realized,
As she was slowly filled with dread.

She was stepping into the real world,
No longer able to be the carefree child she once was when
she was six.
She had to make a name for herself,
Ready to face the universe with all of its cunning little tricks.

She watched from afar first,
As other innocent children occupied the worn-out wooden
swing.
She joined them, hesitantly,
Trying to relive her earliest memory
In hopes it would make her sing.

But she had little glee occupying her soul
And heavy anxiety still taking over her mind;
Her carefree nature and innocence would not be something
she could easily find.

Little did she know that she had to go through a journey for
her inner child to be found;
But until then, her worried state of mind would be where she
would currently be bound.

Diamond

She would not have made it if she were alone.
She knew for a fact that she would not have.

She was not brave enough,
Smart enough,
Funny enough,
Or kind enough to have made it all on her own.

She would not have made it if it was not for the rough diamond
That settled itself within her life.

A diamond that showed her that mistakes were meant to be made,
That lessons had to be learnt.

A diamond that taught her how to be brave enough,
Smart enough,
Funny enough,
And kind enough.
A diamond so beautiful and so utterly rare

That no miner would ever dream to find,
Even if they spent their whole lifetime digging through rocks
And praying for a similar masterpiece to be theirs.

She never took the diamond for granted.
For as long as she remembers,
She kept it polished and safe.
However, life had other plans and the diamond was destined
to be scratched.

A scratch that to others would mar the diamond's beauty,
But to her...
It was still ever so stunning.

She kept the diamond in the palm of her hands whenever she
could
And close to her heart whenever she had to leave it safe at
home.
A diamond in the rough it was,
But a diamond she will always unconditionally love.

Yellow

A ray of sunshine was placed into her life
From the day her eyes blinked open to the world around her.
A beautiful sunflower that bloomed,
From the moment God allowed her to take her first breath.

The winds blew them in opposite directions with age,
But they found their way back to one another.
Each was the others' ray of sunshine,
Every force on earth pulled them back together.

It did not matter that her yellow was her polar opposite,
For no one brought her joy like she did.
Because if the whole world were to close down on her,
She would just wait for her sunflower to flourish and bring
her smile back like a little kid.

God gave them one another to always stay by the others'
side,
God knew that a love and friendship like theirs would be hard
to find.

Moon

She loved spending time with the moon,
The way its light brightened up the darkness around her,
The way its light illuminated the darkness within her.

She loved the moon and all its stages,
Beginning from its birth into a new moon,
To slowly forming into a crescent and becoming ever so full and complete.

She loved the moon because just like the moon and its stages,
She was going through the stages as well,
And a large part of her was ever so grateful to have someone keep her company.

The moon never judged her,
Not when she fell through the deep black hole,
And not when she lost who she was and was no longer in control.

The moon soothed her worries and calmed her soul,
It brought her comfort and, in mere seconds, made her feel
whole.
The moon asked for nothing in return but the company of a
friend,
It was willing to offer its support for its love had no end.

She loved spending time with the moon,
Even when the joys of the world surrounded her.
She loved spending time with the moon
Because time always seemed to pass like a blur.

She loved the moon and all its wonderful stages,
And she will continue loving the moon for the next coming
ages.

Butterfly

A beautiful soul she was when she entered her life,
Peeking out of her cocoon,
Trying to build a friendship after she was wronged by her past.

They walked together,
Hand in hand,
Crossing rivers and mountains,
Celebrating their wins and wiping away one another's sorrows.

They both flourished in their own manner,
Growing together but also growing apart.
She always held the other close to the heart,
For she knew that no soul could replace all they had built from the start.

She should have known though,
That just as her beautiful soul peeked out of her cocoon,
She would one day spread her wings and become a wandering butterfly.

And oh, was she right!

The butterfly flew into a kaleidoscope of butterflies and lost
herself in the crowd.
The butterfly started to mingle with the others and stand
proud.

She watched with a saddened smile as the river of sorrows
pushed them apart.
She knew that she would always wish her love as she did
since the start.
She rejoices in the creature's growth as she flies through the
crowd.
Her heart remains at ease when she sees the butterfly stay
safe and sound.

Now, the butterfly flaps her wings to find her way,
A beautiful soul like hers should not be kept at bay.

Cloud

For as long as she remembered,
She always expected that nothing would go her way;
That the universe was against her in some way.

She stayed in this headspace for years on end;
This terrible habit of hers was not something that anyone
was able to commend.

Alas, she closed the doors on herself for a month or two,
She went to places that no one in the world even knew.
She sat on sandy beaches surrounded by palm trees all
around.
She hoped that at least for a while, she would not be found.

But as she looked up to the sky,
She viewed a cloud creeping towards her.
A twinkle of joy could be viewed in her eye
As a sense of calmness suddenly started to take over her.

It was apparent that it would rain,
But she could not bring herself to care.
She always did love the rain,
The cold droplets on her skin were something she could bear.

The cloud had a habit of taking her anxiety away,
By showering her with droplets of tranquility and keeping
her negative thoughts at bay.
It reminded her of all the wonderful parts of her soul,
It reminded her that she is not one that should ever fall.

She could not imagine a world without the cloud shadowing
her from the world around,
She unconditionally loved the cloud for with it she felt safe
and sound.

She promised herself that she would not allow the smile to
leave her face.
She promised herself that she would always hold her own
soul in a warm embrace.
She would give herself all she ever wanted and more.
She would live in the clouds of joy and forever soar.

Sunstone

Two representations of joy and happiness
Who showed her that dreams were worth fighting for.
Two representations of strength and warmth
Who pushed her to achieve all she wanted and soar.

Life pulls one down at times,
Reaching a state where inspirations and goals are hard to find.
She wallowed in her dull state of mind,
Watching the days pass, not understanding why the universe was not ever so kind.

She wanted to do so much,
But could not bring herself to move.
She wanted to become so great,
But could not find any goal to choose.

She was starting to lose all hope
And decided it might be best to take a couple of steps back.
It seemed like she had to live a mundane and boring life,
But she was not sure if she was meant for that.

Two healing stones that brought her clarity and sense,
They showed her that she had to pull herself out of that state
For her to be able to see through a wider lens.

She was meant for greater things and she knew
That she was able to have it all and slowly pull through.
If the world thought she would fail and burn,
She would simply pull herself up and take it as a lesson to learn.

She was meant to be great and they knew
That a small push is what she needed to breakthrough.

Chapter 2
The First

Love

A small glimmer of hope in a situation
Where darkness is likely to consume everything and anything
Is all it took for her to walk towards him with cautious steps.

Her heart thumped against her rib cage;
Her palms started to sweat, for she was about to engage.
She always thought that he would be hers forever
Because forever is all she ever wanted him to be for her.
She thought that maybe if she stayed close to his side,
He would consume every part of her entire being.

So, she walked.
But then she stopped.

He sat there.
He sat there with the biggest smile decorating his blushed
face.
His eyes crinkled at the sides,
His voice echoed in the hallway,
And his eyes gleamed with love.
He was like she always wanted him to be—happy.

She always thought that she knew how he looked when he was happy,
Yet she forgot one thing;
She never had the chance to see how he looked when he was in love.

It looked breathtaking.
It felt as if someone had placed a large river in the middle of the desert,
As if the entire Milky Way could be seen with all its glories,
And as if the stunted flowers suddenly began blooming.

He loved.
He fell and he chased and he loved.
And she lost.

For he was not looking at her,
But rather he was looking at another.

She was beautiful too.
Like the drop of rain in drought,
Like sunshine on a gloomy day.
She saw him love another,
And all she wanted was for him to listen to her heart—it was painful to hear.
Her selfish heart could not be happy for him.
She wanted to—
Oh god, did she want to—
And she tried so hard.

But she was in so much pain that all she cared about was mending her own heart.

When she mends it,
She will try to let him go.
When she mends it,
She will wish him well.
Yet, for now, she cannot think about anyone but herself,
For she needs to heal before she could think of him.

Falling for him was her mistake.
Keeping the hope alive was her fault.
Trying to keep him was her naivety.
But loving him—was her destruction.

Souls

She begins with similes and metaphors because that is what she is good at.
She puts feelings into paper and pain into ink, and wears her heart on her sleeve.
She looks at the moon and the stars as they mark scars on her heart from afar.

Somewhere, she knew, he was counting the stars with her too.
1, 2, and 20,
Numbers he utters as she listens with her eyes shut and ears open intently.
She listens as if he is beside her,
And there is nothing in the world that could ruin their peace.
She listens as if her heart has not been scarred and crushed
Because she is merely glad to even have his presence in her life.

They found each other when they crossed the narrow sea of innocence and laughter.

Their souls drifted but their minds connected.

She shared her pain,
Her weaknesses,
Her strengths,
And her deepest thoughts.
He shared his happiness,
His experiences,
And what his day brought.

She poured her soul into a bottle and handed it over to him,
But he gave his soul to a shooting star and watched it pass as
a bright hue.

He uttered what was on his mind,
But did not give her his soul.
She uttered what was on her mind and heart,
But she also wrapped all of her soul and gave him everything
that she was, at no cost at all.

That is where she went wrong.

She did not wait to see if he would continue counting the
stars
Until he reached 100, 200, or 500.
She did not wait to see if his shooting star would appear
And him take the chance to grasp it in his palms.
She did not wait to see if he were willing

To ever give her his soul to her the same way she sold hers
without a second thought.

Because if she had waited,
She would have seen that he had no patience
For a soul that was no longer of importance to him.

Their minds were one,
But their souls were far apart.
The narrow sea widened,
Pushing them until they were no longer filled with innocence,
laughter or art.
They became two souls who lost each other along the way.

She thought she deserved him,
And he thought he deserved better.

Hers

Everything was different.
Everything changed after that moment.
The doors opened up,
The tunnels lightened up,
And her heart started to beat again.

Everything was changing.
Everything was going back to the way it used to be.
They could finally soar, they could finally be one, and they could finally love.
Rather more accurately,
She could finally love without breaking apart.

He left the other.
She should not be happy, but she was.
Her selfish nature could never bear seeing him with another.

He was always hers.

He was always the person who turned her world into the most beautiful paradise.

He was always the person who lifted her spirits and made her see a brighter universe.

He was always hers until the other came along.

Then, he was no longer hers.

It hurt.

It really did.

Droplets escaped her hazel eyes.

Eyes that people always said were so big and gleamed with nothing but glee.

She cried day and night because she lost him.

She lost him to someone who probably did not deserve how wonderful he truly was.

He forgot her.

After he got the other, he forgot all about her.

They barely spoke,

He barely laughed,

And they barely opened up to each other.

She missed him.

Every time her eyes would meet his lover's,

Her heart would shatter as if shards of glass had pierced through and made her bleed.

He no longer saw her, but she always saw him.

They completed each other.
Didn't they?
Maybe they didn't.
Maybe he just completed her.

Then, he left the other.
Or maybe she left him.
No matter how it ended,
The outcome was the same, because he came back.
She always believed that she had enough self-dignity
To not open her arms to the people who hurt her,
But she guessed that did not apply to him.

She took him back like nothing had ever changed.
Nothing mattered because he was finally hers again,
And she was finally his.
She was always his though,
But he just never figured it out.

She took him back,
And for now,
She is absolutely glad.
He was the epitome of perfection and her brightest star.
He was the most dangerous thing that has ever greeted her
heart.

Alas, she will love him until the universe explodes and her heart completely shatters.

She will not destroy herself for him,

But he will always have the power to destroy her.

He was all that she ever wanted,

But he was also all that she will never have.

Hurt

He hurt her.
He hurt her so bad to the point where she was close to breaking.

They were like two birds, always soaring with others,
But still protecting each other.
They were like two daises in a field of tulips,
Standing out yet basking in each other's scent.

Though, as years passed,
They fell and they wilted.
They broke and they lost.
They hurt and he left.
He left and she started thinking about how she could have done him wrong.

Did she forget to love him enough?
Was her attention so drawn to herself and her own problems
That she did not search his brown eyes?
Was she so distracted with the world around her

That she could not see the brown changing into a dark pit of
infinite darkness and pain?
What could she have done wrong?

Her heart started to skip beats in the worst way possible.
She lost hope in herself because she could not for the life of
her find the answer.

Everything changed.
They grew and they blossomed.
They searched and they learned.

They became two different people with filled hearts.
Her heart was filled with love and hatred,
Kindness and anger,
Selflessness and greed.
His heart was filled with …
She would not know.

She was unaware of who he was anymore.

She always had this mesmerizing image of him in her head;
The perfect human to have ever graced her life.
To this day, that is how she always saw him as.

Whether he was cruel and selfish,
Or loving and generous,
Her weak heart would not care.
For her heart did not care about how he hurt it in the past;

Thus, it would not care about who he has turned into today.
Her weak heart will always beat for him.

So, in an alternate universe,
If he ever asks her to be his,
Her heart would answer in a heartbeat.

She would fall into the hands of her organ
And allow it to carry her to the future that awaits them with him.
Her poor weak heart would not understand what it was putting itself through;
However, she would understand.
She would understand but would simply let it all go and welcome her ultimate ruin.

Rain

She took a deep breath.
She inhaled with her eyes shut and took in everything around her.
The smell of the rain,
The scent of the trees,
And him.

He stepped closer to her,
As the drops hit her skin and slowly trickled their way down,
And he smiled for the first time in years.

She missed him.

For it had been so long since she had seen his face,
And she could not believe that her eyes had laid upon him once again.

He left without any last words,
And she waited for the universe to take its natural course and bring them together again.

And it did.

The universe planned it perfectly
Because they were now both standing where she fell in love
over and over again—
Under the rain.

Did he not remember her love for the rain?
Did he not remember when she sat in between a thousand
dandelions as the rain drenched her?
He stood there as the biggest laugh vibrated through his
body,
And that was when she realized that something could finally
compete with the sound of the rain.

As time flew by,
She put him first.
She always put him first.

He completed her like no one ever did.

He made flowers bloom inside her chest,
And butterflies flutter in her stomach.
He turned her whole world upside down in the best way
humanely possible.

But then he left.

He left and her entire being was shattered,

For she solely depended on him for the longest time.

The only excuse she heard was that he wanted to figure his
life out,
But the only thing she saw was that he wanted to figure his
life out with another.

She pursued him and let go of her peace
She pursued him and did not think to fend for herself in this
cruel world.
She thought she would finally be his,
But she forgot that it was not yet her time to belong to
someone.

So, for now, she will bask under the rain.
She will breathe it in,
Even as he was standing in front of her,
With his scent clearly trying to take over her senses.

She will breathe in the rain,
And she will fall in love with it,
Over and over again.

Why?

Why did he not love her back?
Was she not good enough for him?
Did she care for him more than she should have?
Did she comfort him more than what she was supposed to?
Was she always too present when he needed her?

Why did he not love her back?
Her heart had so much to give,
And she gave it all to him.

She was the jewel he spent his whole life looking for.
She was already in the palm of his hands and he took her for
granted.
She was his wealth and his pride,
And she was a rarity.
She was willing to be his beginning and his end.
So, she let him possess her.

Why did he not love her back?
She stayed with him through the nights.

She was the owl that did not sleep

Just so she made sure that he was closing his eyes with a smile gracing his lips.

She was the voice that calmed his nerves

And wiped his nightmares away until his worries vanished.

She sacrificed her peace just so he would be at ease.

Why did he not love her back?

Maybe it was her fault.

She saw everyone around her drifting apart from each other,

So she rushed to the glue and tried to keep them together.

She squeezed and squeezed until she was out of glue

And all she could do was sit and wait for it to dry.

She fixed them.

She fixed them before they could break.

Maybe that was her mistake.

Why did he not love her back?

Because she cared for him too much,

Loved him too much,

Stayed with him for too long,

And realized her love for him a little too late.

He could no longer see her as his by the time her heart started to beat for him.

It was too late.

Why did he not love her back?

Because, ironically,

He did not fully understand his heart until there was no longer any hope for her at all.

Chapter 3
The Inevitable

Bubble

She was stuck in a colorful bubble,
Never wanting to leave.

Colors were swirling in front of her eyes
And a thousand birds were fluttering in the clear blue sky.
The transparency of everything around her felt like a
whirlwind of fantasies and serenities;
It was a peace she had not felt before.
Yet, in a sudden, her view was darkened by his shadow,
And she stood there in awe.

He was the epitome of perfection.
Her heart skipped a beat,
And she held on to the little amount of sanity she had left.

His eyes drew her in,
And their color made her shiver in anticipation for what they
held.
His smile enthralled her soul,
For it held a level of sincerity that she had never seen before.

In that moment,
She knew she was captivated beyond return.

His entire being captivated her.
It captivated her to the point where she was ready to destroy
the bubble she lived in for him.

She wanted to feel his face under her palm.
She wanted to slowly run her fingers over every feature,
Every line, every crevice,
Every perfection and imperfection.

He brought her sanity, and he held her in her palms.
He opened her eyes to the world around her.
She started to realize that the bubble she lived in
Showed her the smallest part of this beautiful world,
But he showed her the eternal universe.

She craved his company, his voice, and his very existence.
She craved his heartbeat beneath her fingers and his eyes
faithfully holding hers.

She fell for him as if he were her source of air,
For she could not believe that she found something so rare.

Flames

He was not unapproachable; he was anything but.
He was everything that people wanted to be with and wanted to become,
And he knew it from the start.
He was a dangerous flame that was never put out,
And they were ignorant moths that were drawn to his light.

They knew what he was capable of;
They knew of the pain he could cause.
Yet, with eyes wide open,
They spiraled towards his light and went down in flames.

You would think they would learn.
You would think that after their wings had been shredded,
And their organs stopped functioning
That they would realize how harmful his heat was.

But they never do.

They regenerate themselves,

Thinking maybe the second time around everything will change
Because we live in a world where change is ideal,
But they start spinning in circles as it happens again.

She never approached him.
She was smart enough not to.
But that did not mean that she did not flutter around his light.

She flew around the flame carefully,
Tentatively,
Afraid of getting too close
Because if she ever got too close,
She was afraid that she would never come back.
She was afraid that she would not be capable of regenerating herself,
As she was putting herself at harm's way all over again.

If she ever got too close,
She was afraid that he would notice her colorful nature and drag her into his never-ending flame.

She did not think that she would ever be able to leave then,
Even though she knew that he would offer nothing but a slow, painful burn.

Hence, she continued to flutter around him at a distance,
Gazing at his changing colors from afar,

But fearing to close the distance between their attractive natures.

She was a butterfly who had yet to discover the world,

And he had all the power to trap her in his scorching hold.

Dust

He never actually wanted her,
But he loved the idea of having her.
He did not run to her when she was standing at the end of
the tunnel with her arms wide open,
Ready to give him every part of her that she kept buried deep
within.
He kept his distance as the dark fog engulfed her
And turned her into smoke and dust.

He was once the biggest part of her infinite galaxy,
And she was once the smallest but brightest star in his heart.
He took her for granted and she slowly felt like falling apart.

Though, she realized that she was once his star
And that could one day make her someone else's entire
galaxy.
For she never thought that someone could shed him away
from her mind,
And that was what made the situation oh so pleasant.
Yet, the best part about this humorous globe that we live in
is that we are always proven wrong.

She was held in a captivating stare,
And her heart swelled at the turned tables.
She was no longer just a star or a galaxy,
But rather the entire universe and its eternal depth.
She captivated another and he slowly became an uncontrollable flame.

It was a humorous game to him,
And he hated coming out last.
His competitive nature wanted to play,
And he pressed the button over and over again.

Yet, when you lose something once,
Gain it back,
And decide to take it for granted again,
It has a tendency of seeing its worth.

Unfortunately for her,
It was not her turn to be enlightened.

Pain

She felt it the moment it happened; it was like nothing she had felt before.
Her hands trembled and her lips parted in shock.
Her eyes watered and her heart threatened to stop.
He stuck the blade in her chest and turned it slowly, painfully, and willingly.

He killed every cell in her body and expected her to forget.
He broke every bone in her and she was left for dead.

It slowly dawned upon her that she was never his prized aurora that she believed was put in his course of life.
She never beautified his world like he claimed she did.

She remembered when she first met him,
And she swore that she had never seen someone as breathtaking.

Every fiber in her being told her to not get too close to him,
But she did,
And oh, was she a fool.

She approached, and he took the extra step,
And then they became one.

He said that they were royalty,
Never to be touched,
But always to be admired from afar.
They were constellations that formed an image of perfection
and pure love.

Pure love.

Their love was pure.
That was what he used to tell her.
Their love was so pure that they feared hurting each other.

Then why did he turn her world into a battle of emotions?
Not knowing whether to love him wholeheartedly or despise
his very existence.

He crushed her in a matter of seconds.
He made her stand in front of a thousand people as he turned
the knife with ease.

It was never real.
None of it was real.

His love, his heart,
His honest eyes,
And the whispers that left his lips – they were never real.

He was never real.

He was never hers,
And she was never his.

She was never his aurora because he never could see what beauty was.

He was so blinded by the satisfaction of being able to crumble her heart
That he forgot how he was fooling himself.
He caused her pain,
But nothing could compare to the pain he caused himself
When he let her go.

Maybe

Maybe if her waist was thinner,
Maybe if her chest was bigger,
Maybe if her arms were smaller,
Maybe then she would be enough.

Maybe if her lips were plumper,
Maybe if her eyelashes were longer,
Maybe if her nose was smaller,
Maybe then she would be enough.

Maybe if her hair was thicker,
Maybe if her smile was wider,
Maybe if her stomach was flatter,
Maybe then she would be enough.

Maybe if her voice was softer
Maybe if she was a little smarter,
Maybe if she was a bit taller,
Maybe then she would be enough.

Maybe if she changed herself,

She would finally feel enough
Because for the longest time,
The demons made a home for themselves in her head
And made it ever so tough.

She ran her fingers over her face,
And imagined the marking pens leaving their trace.
She could become a different person in a day,
She would finally be enough and all her doubts would go
away.

All the maybes of the world filled her restless mind,
Making her deaf to all the beauty in her and leaving her blind.
But she forgot one maybe,
The most honest of them all;
One maybe,
That could rescue her from her own downfall.

Maybe if the world was kinder,
Not one soul would feel worthless.
Maybe if the world was kinder,
All these thoughts would not make her feel so restless.

Red

She met someone new.
Someone new, but maybe he'd color her blue.
He splashed her with words like rainbows and stardust.
He became the sky at sunset that made her dulled heart fill
with lust.

He took her into his arms,
And showed her that love was worth fighting for.
He took her into his arms
And told her that as long as he was hers,
They could risk everything and anything.

But she was not willing to go that far.

She was scared.
She was afraid that they would become one
And she would not love him like he would want her to.
She was afraid that they would fall apart and she would scar
him.
For even if she hurt herself more than she hurt him,

His heart should not be the one left scarred.
His heart was too pure for her.

They were light and dark,
But he could not see it.
He thought that she was the light in his life,
And he was the light in hers.

But he was wrong.

She still was not able to witness any light surrounding her.
Her thoughts were a mess,
Her heart was erratic,
And her soul was shadowed.

He thought he found his match,
But she knew that she would light him up and burn him in
the flames.
Because although he surrounds her with his light,
She only beautifies him for a while.

He needs his sun,
But all she is and ever will be is his moon.
For he is red, and she is grey,
Yet he needs his yellow, and she needs her blue.
The sky at sunset could never be breathtaking without the
sun.

Sealed

She broke his heart when he was willing to give it all to her.

He took cautious steps towards her,
Like a baby concentrating on his very first steps.
He opened up to her and made her feel like a flower that was
ready to bloom.
He told her to speak from her heart and to stop listening to
her brain.
He told her to not think and simply speak as if her words were
an unstoppable falling star.

But she could not,
Or rather she would not.

Her heart was fragile.
She had already sealed it shut a while back,
And she was not willing to tear it open just yet.

She was well reserved in her words,
In her thoughts,

In her actions,
And he knew.
It was easy for him to figure her out.

She was an open book to him.
He listed her traits one after the other.
He accepted her flaws and welcomed her storm,
Even if he did not view them as flaws.

He told her he wanted her.
He told her he wanted to love her
And have her love him back.
And hearing that hurt because she knew
She could not give him what he was asking from her.
But she knows it did not hurt her as much as it hurt him,
And for that she weeps.
It was never her intention to hurt him,
But she also cannot lead him on when she has barely figured
herself out.

Maybe she will one day regret letting him go.
Maybe she will learn to speak from her heart and break the
seal.
Maybe she will be willing to give someone her heart and
more.
But for now,
She cries for hurting him,
For he did not deserve a girl with a heart that had been
locked in a cage.

Heart

It was the first time she felt such joy.

She heard words that she never thought she would hear.
She heard melodies and symphonies and her heart skipped many beats.
She heard words that put a lump in her throat because she was not expecting them.
She heard words that made butterflies dance in her stomach every time she remembered them.
She heard words that she always hoped she would hear but she never did.
At least not until now.

They were two strangers who met and never paid much attention to one another.
They kept meeting by chance and they never saw how much they meant to the other.
They yelled and smiled,
Fought and laughed,
Loved and kept it buried within their hearts.

She went to others,
But so did he.
Yet, they always found our way back to each other.

They laughed as if that night was their last.
His lips poured out sweet words as if he would no longer have another chance.
She opened her heart as if she and he were made for each other.
Then, he told her he loved her,
And everything became quiet.
She could hear his heartbeat and hers beat in sync,
But that was the only thing she could hear.

He loved her,
And it hurt him to utter the words because he was afraid of losing her.
He did not want to let go of her,
And she did not want to let go of him too because she loved him.

She loved him,
But her fear of losing him was stronger than the hold her heart had on her.
So, she asked him to forget.
She asked him to erase that night
Because she did not think her heart was strong enough to lose him.
And he did.

Why did it hurt though?

She asked him to forget,

So why did it hurt that he did?

Why did it hurt that he acted as if nothing happened between them?

She knew one day, everything will fall into place and it will make sense,

But she cannot wait for that day.

She loved him.

She loved him and everything about him.

She loved him,

And it is a pity that she did not realize it sooner.

Fear

It was something she had never experienced before.
She was not an expert, but she claimed to be one.
She claimed to know about everything that revolved around
this experience,
But she was wrong.

She met him.

She met him and he was the first person she decided to open
her heart to.
She listened to him when his heart bled,
And she argued and left him with everything he said.
But she always came back to him because he was her first.

He was the first person her heart decided to get attached to.
But then, everything fell apart.

They came crashing down.

They fell like stars when their life span comes to an end.

They fell like two birds with broken wings that could no longer be fixed.
She fell, but he had fallen a while back;
She just did not enjoy accepting it.

He kept his distance and tried to look for someone else to help him
Because she did not heal him and give him what his heart desired.

She was broken,
And she wanted to be fixed.
Her heart was made of glass,
And she was naïve enough to have given it to him.

She tried getting him back,
But he was too busy pursuing his first love.

So, she sat and tried to glue the shards back together.
Yet, even when her heart was fixed, it was still scarred.

Her wings were broken.
Her thoughts were somewhere else.
And her heart could not be mended.
She was going through an inner battle with herself
And she still felt that she would not end up winning.

She was filled with fear.
She was scared that she would break her own heart.

She was scared that she would not be able to forget her first

Nor will she be able to let him go.

She feared that she would destroy herself.

She was afraid.

She is afraid.

Hail

He came into her life as if he were the hail that her heart had been waiting for.

It began with tiny droplets of rain,
Cascading down her skin,
Covering every inch of flesh and bone.

It felt peaceful and exciting,
As if the entire drought that marred her heart was slowly vanishing.
She closed her eyes and allowed her brain to lead her
Because her heart was too vulnerable at that moment.

The rain grew stronger and louder,
And she and he grew closer and closer.
The water pricked against her skin and it hurt for a second,
But after that, it became her favorite feeling in the world.

Their conversations grew deeper,
And his significance to her grew stronger.
Her brain moved forward,
But her heart was already three steps ahead.

Yet, the rain continued pricking and pricking;
It would not stop.
Her brain and heart stopped functioning properly.
She could not see that the rain's intention was to harm her,
So she continued looking forward to the feeling.

She began understanding.
She slowly, but surely, started to realize that the rain did not
want to fill her heart with joy.
The rain did not want her to close her eyes and await a better
tomorrow.
The rain did not want to make her happy.

The rain wanted to cause her pain and make her suffer.
So, the rain turned into hail,
And she started to fall as it fell upon her skin.
She fell as it fell and pierced through her heart.

It was all a game.
None of it was real.

She was supposed to put her arm out and cherish the feeling
in her hand.
It was supposed to feel nice.

It was supposed to feel whimsical and magical.
The rain was supposed to feel good,
The hail was supposed to feel new and out of this world.
They were 'supposed' to.

But they did not.

They hurt.
They hurt her.
She fell for what they presented to this world,
And she failed to see the harm they presented her with,
The harm he presented her with.

Lost

Not a day can pass by without his name securing itself in her head.

She cannot seem to get him out of her thoughts,

And she did not know if that is a curse or a blessing.

Some days it felt great,

Simply hearing his name in her head made her heart flutter.

Other days it felt dreadful

Because simply hearing his name built a fear in her heart that could not be tamed.

At times,

The words that left her lips prevented her from thinking.

She felt as if her brain could not form a single sentence,

No matter how hard she tried.

Her entire being changed when she was with him,

And for the first time,

She felt as if she was no longer in control of her own body.

She did not know whether she should have felt free or imprisoned by him.

He kept saying that her presence comforted him,
And she believed him.
Yet, when she was no longer in control of herself,
She could not figure out if her naivety had taken over or not.

For the first time,
She could not seem to trust her gut.
He had utterly and completely made her feel lost.
She lost herself in the clouds after she met him.

He may be her new beginning or her own personal end.
He may completely change her to the best or make her forget who she was.
He may fully take over her heart or slowly and painfully hurt her soul over and over again.
Yet, being lost had never felt as euphoric as it did when she was with him.

Attached

She gets attached too often.
She listened to her heart for months,
And she could not foresee the tragedy that was about to unfold.
She thought that they would end,
But she forgot that she was someone who could not let people go easily.
So, she held her ground.

She did not leave,
But that was mainly because she did not want to.
She fooled herself into thinking that it was him who was hung up on her,
But it was always her who was hung up on him.

His voice was like a melody to her ear.
It was not the most wonderful,
But it was her favorite.

His laugh opened up windows in her chest that she thought
would stay shut for a while.
She had her heart sheltered inside her chest,
Fearing getting hurt once again.
Yet, she forgot to guard it when he decided to enter her life.

As the moments passed,
She grew more attached.
As she listened to him more,
Her heart slowly started feeling again.

She panicked.
She panicked and held her breath.
She panicked and held her heart.
She panicked and broke apart.

She did not want to feel again.
She did not want to hurt again.
She did not want to love again.
She did not want to.
She was not strong enough to.

She was not strong enough to feel something for him
When she knew that he would never feel the same way for
her.
She was not strong enough to experience an unrequited love
And stay because she would not be able to bring herself to
let go.

She was not strong enough to stop her heart again like she
did once before.

He could never feel something for her,
And she did not think she could let him go anytime soon.
It was too late.
Her heart had already left its cage,
And she did not have enough strength to lock it up again.

So, she once again hurt herself willingly,
But she could not bring herself to care.
Because for now, he is all she has.
And for now, he is all she wants.

Snow

A white blanket surrounded her as she looked around.
Pure and cold,
Yet breathtakingly beautiful.
The snow reached her ankles as she stared into the distance,
Expecting nothing but also everything at the same time.

She never thought that he would secure a place in her heart
as he has today.
She never thought that she would ever be able to reach the
level of peace that she has reached now with him in her
arms.

They say that the smallest particle of dust can mar the purity
of snow.
It can turn its whiteness to any of the other colors in the
spectrum.
It can prove that perfection does not exist,
That purity is merely a figure of people's imagination.
That is what she thought as well as the days passed with him
by her side.

When she met him,
The blanket that surrounded him was dark and frightening.
When she met him,
Her sanity started to leave her.
Yet, as time ticked by,
She came to realize that maybe she should let go
Because she was not getting what she was looking for from
him.

Her whole life fell into a pit of darkness
Because she expected something from him that she should
not have.
And when she realized her mistake,
Every little dust started lifting itself from the white coat
around him.

She expected something from him that she should not have.
She forced things that she should not have forced.
So, she allowed fate to take its course as she watched from a
distance.
She stood mesmerized as each dust particle was lifted off.
She stood in awe as everything around her turned white.

She had a tendency to create a false image of those who
stepped into her life,
Placing them on a pedestal that they were never worthy of.
She marred the purity of the snow with her delusions
And questioned in surprise as to why the particles existed.

She was too naïve.

Too young.

It is a pity that she realized it a little too late

Numb

A wise person once told her that when one knows that she is feeding herself lies,
It is time to accept the truth,
Because not doing so will hurt a thousand times more in the end.
The wise person was her,
And she weeps for not listening to herself.

When they met,
She promised herself that she would hold her heart back.
She lied and told herself that she would not allow things to develop.
She lied and told herself that she would not let herself feel,
But she did.

She felt,
And she wished that she had not.

She poured her heart out.
She grew attached.

She worried,
She asked,
She cried,
She smiled,
She yelled,
And she felt.

Once again, she felt that she could no longer depend on her instincts.

She was lost,
And she did not think that she wanted to be found.

She suddenly felt as if she could lose him.
It was ironic how even though he should have been afraid of losing someone who cared for him,
It was actually her who was afraid to lose someone who could not care less about her.

Yet, she felt numb.
She no longer felt alive.

She walked down the streets,
Passing every person with a blank slate in her head.
She faked a smile to every wandering eye.
She faked a laugh to every attentive ear.
She became someone who she could no longer recognize,
But she knew that she could not lie to herself anymore.
She loved him.

She utterly,
Completely,
And faithfully loved him.
But she wished that she did not.

She could no longer live a lie,
Not when she felt his presence in her life.
If only she had listened and stepped on her heart,
It would not hurt as much.

Yet, she loves him,
And it is a pity that she cannot seem to love anyone but him.
What the heart wants,
The heart gets,
And if the heart wants to be torn to shreds,
So be it.

Stars

We spend years looking up at the sky,
Hoping to figure out the days that were yet to come,
Hoping that the stars will rain down all the answers we were
looking for.

We spend so much time rushing into things
In order to experience feelings that were not supposed to be
felt yet.

But everything has its own time and place.

The stars never made sense to her.
She kept looking at them for hours
And she never understood why she felt the way she did.

They never told her why she was so afraid to love.
Or rather, why she was so afraid to admit that she was in
love.
Could it be that she was afraid to lose those she loved?
But what if they loved her back?

Would she get over her fear?
She did not think she would.

She will never be able to tell him that she loves him.
Not when her eyes pour rain,
Not when short breaths escape her lips,
And not when her legs give out from exhaustion.
She will never bring herself to admit it to him.

Maybe they were destined for one another.
Maybe that is why he had not yet left her life
Even as she wished upon every star to soothe her heart and
aid in letting him go.

Yet, she still would not tell him.

For even if a small part of her believes that they are destined
for one another,
She knows that he already made up his mind about who he
is destined to be with.
And that person is not her.

She will never admit to falling in love.
The stars could threaten to burst right before her very eyes
so she would submit,
But she still would not utter a word.
She would rather hurt alone than hurt in front of another.
She would rather love in secrecy than admit and face an
unrequited love.

Destroy

Fire and gasoline,
That is what they were.
She was a bursting flame,
And he came to light her up and cause her to self-destruct.

He promised to destroy her.
He promised to make her burn.
She just did not think he was speaking the truth.

He took her into his arms and warmed her soul.
She closed her eyes and ravished in the feelings she experienced with him,
As his warmth seeped through her veins.
Again, he promised he would burn her ongoing fire,
But she did not think that was possible.

Her heart started beating.
Her foolish heart was ready again.
So, she let go.
She let herself get attached.

She craved the poison.
She craved how she lit up more and more
Every time he came close to her.

He wanted her.
He said that he would destroy her,
But he also said that he wanted her.

But he wanted to burn her and turn her to ashes.
He wanted to leave nothing of her but a pile of dust.

He lied.

All his words were lies.
He never cared for her,
He never loved her,
And he never wanted her.
But he was honest about one thing.
He would destroy her.
He would kill her heart.

Because he was not gasoline,
She just thought he was.
He was the vacuum that took all the oxygen and killed her
flame.

He kept his promise because in his eyes,

She was the perfect contender for destruction.

She let herself be played once again.

But a fool should not expect her fire to stay alive

When she had already been warned that she was bound to

die.

Used

She was an object of comfort.
An object of pleasure,
But an object of comfort.

She allowed herself to be whisked into the thunderstorm that was him,
And she was torn into shreds from the inside out.
She was taken into him and it was like nothing she had experienced before.
She felt her eyes open up to all the new things that were spiraling her way,
And there was no way she could have stopped it.

It was like ecstasy.
It was like a drug that she had never consumed before,
And it was so exhilarating trying it for the first time.

He taught her how to see things in a different perspective.

He complicated her life in a way that no one had.

He spun her around along with all the other people
Who had fallen into his storm and could not escape.
But he could not touch her.
He could only kill her from afar.

He fed on them.
He consumed them.
He brought himself peace through her,
And maybe the others too.

He claimed that there were no others,
But she could see them spinning.
They were drained and being suffocated
As the air was pulled out from their lungs.
But it did not matter to him.
He was emotionally satisfied,
Even if it was for a short period of time.

She was being used for the comfort of his heart.
She felt it.
Her heart felt it.
She was too fragile and he knew it.
He knew she was weak
But he still decided to swallow her up into his storm.

She was ruined.
She was emotionally numb.
She could no longer see what was in front of her.
She could no longer distinguish what her heart wanted.

She could no longer feel anything for anyone.

His storm swallowed her whole.
He killed the love that was in her heart.
He seeped through her veins and she was suddenly high on him,
And she was content.

She knew she was being used,
But she ignored it because he made everything new to her.

She tore herself apart with her own bare hands,
And she did not even realize it until it was too late.

Time

It did not feel pleasant knowing that she was being used.

It did not feel pleasant knowing that she never meant anything

To someone who meant the world to her.

It made her think whether she was blind

To all the mistakes that she witnessed before her eyes

Because she could not have been that shallow to not have seen them from the start.

A part of her always knew that he was using her,

But she could never figure out what for.

A part of her was always aware that she cared for him more than he did for her,

But she could never understand why.

She was blind but she was not ignorant,

For she knew of his true nature,

But she chose to ignore it for the sake of her own heart.

He loved another,

And that was fine because she knew that she and him could never be.
She was just a spare toy he played with
Whenever his favorite toy did not function as he wanted it to.

She cared,
She listened,
She laughed,
And she even loved,
Yet she wished that she had not.

Then, when his favorite toy was obedient again,
She was left to pick herself up and carry her fragile heart on her own.

Hearing him tell her that she changed, humored her.
Hearing him tell her that she no longer cared, appalled her.
But then again,
He never saw any wrong in what he did.

She did not lose him,
But rather he lost her.
She was not just a wandering figure in his life,
And one day,
He will figure that out.

Third

A small part of her was still alive after all this time.
A small part of her heart was still beating.
A small part of her soul still lived as the sun set
And the moon replaced it every night.
Foolishly, she gave what was left of her to him.

She gave him all she had left because she trusted
That he would never hurt her like they did.
She gave him her heart and she never asked for anything in
return.

He was her muse,
Her sapphire,
And her last hope.
She expected everyone to step over her rare heart
But she could have never thought that he would be one of
them.

He met another and he distanced herself from her.
He slowly moved her,
His precious jewel,
To the side to make place for his new toy on the shelf.
He slowly pushed her to the back of his mind and brought the
other right to the front.

Yet, she accepted it;
She should not have,
But she did.
She still could not have expected what was to come.

On the 3rd of the 20th,
She lost what was left of herself.
He pushed her to the ground in order to make the other
happy.
Tears poured from her eyes and he heard her scream and
yell,
As if she was holding on for dear life,
Afraid of losing the small part of him that was left for her.

On the 3rd of the 20th,
She died.
She had no one left to hold on to.
Her heart could no longer care to beat anymore.
Her soul could no longer bear staying in her body any longer.

On the 3rd of the 20th,
He killed the only person who never scarred him.

On that day,
He stepped over the purest soul that entered his life
And turned her into a walking corpse.
On that day,
He destroyed the greatest thing that had ever happened to
him.

She hoped it was worth it.

Limit

She handled more mistakes than she could count.
She handled more mistakes than a sane human being could
have put up with.

She put him on the highest pedestal her heart allowed her
to.

She gave him the sky,
The moon,
And all the stars along with it.

Never did it cross her mind that it was time to hurt him,
And never did it cross her mind that it was time to let him go.
Yet, every person reaches a point in life where they are ready
to free fall.

She recognized all of his mistakes,
She was quiet with every hurtful gesture towards her,
And she braced herself for all the others to come.
Yet, all of his mistakes were the same;

Mistakes that she had already familiarized herself with.
Thus, she expected them every once in a while.
But he loved surprising her, did he not?

He left the biggest show of all for last.
He decided to perform when she was at her happiest,
When she had already accepted his distance
And had become numb to all his past mistakes.

He performed his act and pushed her past her limit.
He decided to ruin her when she thought she was finally at
peace.

It was her fault for loving him more than loving herself.
She loved him more than she loved all those who entered
And left her life in a blink.
Yet, with all the mistakes,
Never once did she think that she could pack her heart and
leave,
But there is a first time for everything.

He pushed her past the line that she had set for him,
And she finally had the courage to let him go.

He made her leave when she was willing to stay.

He made her go when she was willing to be hurt slightly more.

He made her hate when she was willing to love.

But he also made her love herself when she was ready and willing to let herself go.

Chapter 4
The Rebirth

Grey

She did not want to be in this place anymore.

She no longer had the energy to endure putting herself
Through this process of not knowing what was going to
happen next.

He made everything blurry to her eyes.
He made her drown in this sea of obscurity,
Unable to raise herself to the surface in order to breathe.

Being in this place suffocated her;
It made despise the unknown and all that would come with
it.

Being with him drained every ounce of energy left in her.
He was never able to articulate what he wanted from the
people he kept close to him.
He had a tendency to attach to their skin and leech on to
them,

Draining all that was left of them then throwing them into the unknown.

He changed the colorful world they saw
Into a dull black and white portrait that left them to fend for themselves with their own thoughts.

Trying to understand what was going on between them
Was like being stuck in a grey area,
Unable to escape,
Unable to go back to all the colors,
Unable to understand how grey was the only color she could see.
It was mentally wearing having to think about
How she could save herself and no longer contemplate about what she meant to him.

She no longer wanted to see the world as a never-ending grey portrait.
She wanted to take a step forward into the white or move her feet back and fall into the black.

If she was unable to see colors anymore,
She would rather fall into the bright light or be swallowed by the darkness behind her.
It would not matter what the outcome would be;
All that would matter would be that she would finally have some sense of clarity.

Ocean

She wants to be swallowed whole by the ocean
Because she no longer knows who she is anymore.
She wants to allow the waves to have their way with her and fill her lungs.
She wants her screams to die down and her tears to be washed away.
She has reached the verge of insanity and it seems way too difficult to turn back.

To be a creature of the ocean seems all too pleasing of a thought.
Being able to communicate and pour her heart out
Can only be viewed as air bubbles rising to the top of the ocean from the bottom within.
Life would be a matter of fighting for survival and finding her way to safety.
The thought seemed awfully addicting.

She could not blame anyone but herself for reaching the brink of insanity.

All along,
She knew what she was getting herself into.
All along,
She knew that she would only bring herself pain by
continuing down this road.

Yet, she never expected her heart to hurt this bad.

She never expected that she would stay late nights gasping
for air,
Clutching her chest,
And not even wiping her tears because they would pour
down regardless.

Life was too dirty for people like her.
Life was too stained for people who give their all
To make others feel at ease but receive nothing in return.

Drowning in the ocean and having the waves surround her
skin rests her heart.
It brings her erratic heart to a slow beating rhythm,
A rhythm that only continues in order to keep her alive,
Not to help her feel.
It was only a matter of time until her lungs fill up and her
heart becomes void.

Snake

She walked the streets with the breeze brushing through her
hair
She received stares left and right,
But she could not bring herself to care.
She knew they were staring at her battered naked feet;
Or maybe they were looking at the scars marring her arms.

She resurfaced after a period of locking herself up,
Claiming that she was finally reborn into who she was
supposed to be.
She drowned herself in darkness and reshaped her mind,
body and soul.
A broken doll she became and she wanted to break everyone
And watch them fall.

As she was latched onto once,
She sunk her teeth into the others and satisfied her soul.
She relished in the idea that she held all the power;
That no human could break her or ever make her crawl.
Ego is a funny thing, isn't it? Oh—indeed it is.

A slithering snake made its way into her life,
Crawling up her legs and wrapping its body around her waist.
It creeped up her neck and passed through her ear,
Taking in all her insecurities and doubts and nesting its home within.

The snake released its poison,
And that is where the game started.

All who she now was and all who she became
Were slowly turning into a fragile child,
Seeking the approval of others,
Unable to have an ounce of confidence in themselves.

She did not break as she did years back,
But she was rather bitten and scarred,
Beaten and marred.

The cunning reptile understood that she had a long way to go,
That she had yet to reshape herself to the fullest extent.
It knew where her weak spots were,
It knew that she would not fall in love with its poisonous nature,
So it had to look for different ways to satisfy itself.

But she escaped.
She had to,
Or else she would have fallen.

So, she walked down the street
With the dirty concrete staining her blood covered feet,
Looking for an escape,
Looking to be set free,
Looking for a band aid to mend all the scars she had.

She was willing to walk to the depths of the earth to find
herself again,
But it's a pity that she trapped herself in a circle of ignorance
just to feel ounces of bliss,
Time and time again.

Bird

She had her head in the clouds and the world beneath her
feet,
Flying aimlessly amongst the crowd but still feeling
incomplete.
She had the weight of the world on her shoulders,
But the wings of an angel carved into her back.
She had and she had;
What's the point on dwelling on that?

She was looking for an escape,
For a hand from the skies above.
She looked up to God,
And prayed for a sign that would show her any form of love.
She waited for days but to no amends.
She would wake up tomorrow and try once again.

Somewhere amongst the fluff, she saw a bird flutter his
wings.
She turned her head and decided not to entertain his needs.
But a stubborn bird he was, as he tried to pull her in,
And a weak angel she was, as she fell for it again.

He was something out of the ordinary, she realized,
Something she had not experienced before.

He was warm and gentle,
Kind with a heart not made of stone.

He handled her with care,
As if she was bound to break.
He made her see how precious she was,
And she did not think that a few days would be all it would take.

She started to see that kindness was and is all she deserved
For her walls to be torn down and for her to flourish to her highest extent.

She had lived for the longest time with a wall around her heart,
Defenses held high up in order to not open any scars.
He made her realize that she could live being as soft as she was internally,
And made her witness that she could showcase her elegance and confidence gracefully.

He rejuvenated the love she once had for herself and made it stay,
And he showed her that affection is not harshness in any form of way.
Affection is not anger, hurt or loud noises.
Affection is gentleness, love and hushed voices.

The weight on her shoulder felt ever so light,
And the incompleteness she felt was no longer in sight.

Though, as she reached her truest potential,
He decided to take a step back.
He fluttered his blue wing and went down a different path.

She waited to see if he would ever come back.
But he never did,
And she had to live with that.

Yet, she could not bring herself to be mad,
Not even for a little while
Because for the shortest time,
He was the only one who could make her smile.

An angel he was when he entered her life,
Even though he left like a crow when he walked out of her
life.
He still made her see the softest parts of herself
Which were buried deep within,
Hidden from everyone else.

She spent her days looking for a blue bird in the sky,
For the glimmers of softness and hope that once entered her
life.

Blue

She always looked for love in the wrong places;

In dark hearts and wicked faces.

She held hands that let go when it was no longer convenient

for them;

Leaving her behind as if she was not a rare and astonishing

gem.

She was fooled so many times,

Broken for uncommitted crimes.

Her soul was stolen by greedy hands,

And she was forced to give into all their unfair demands.

But she decided it was time to walk away,

To choose herself and no longer stay.

She stepped onto the train headed far away into bliss

Because she finally found peace;

You could see it in her eyes, for it was hard to miss.

She chose to ignore all the chaos around her,
To remove herself from all the things that ever caused her
pain.
She chose all the things that brought tranquility to her,
And it was the first time in so long that she ever felt so sane.
A small bird was all she needed to make her see that the
world
Was more than useless chatter and mindless games.
The world had so much to offer,
All she had to do was take the first step to change.

She spent her years looking for her blue,
Wondering if she was ever bound to find what would
complete her ever graying soul.
Ironically, she was looking in all the wrong places,
For her blue was not that far away at all.

She was not grey;
She was anything but.
She was magenta, turquoise, burgundy, amber,
And all the colors the spectrum had to offer and more.
All she needed was to realize that she,
As she is,
Is a complete being.

And with that being said,
She found her blue.